A Note to Students

This book has been designed to give you a solid understanding of the four basic thumb position fingering patterns. In the first part of the book, each section deals with one pattern. The pieces in the last section have a variety of patterns in them. It will be up to you to figure out which ones to use!

Please follow your teacher's instruction about playing in thumb position. Here, though, is a summary of some important points to observe:

• Let the side of your thumb lie across two (and only two) strings.

• Keep your thumb in a natural, loose "straight" position. Your thumb should neither bow backward nor bend at the first joint. Both of these things usually indicate tension -- which you should avoid at all costs.

• Use the weight from your back to stop the strings. Be careful that your fingers do not poke down into the string causing the knuckles to stick up. Your hand shape should be curved and the base knuckles should be soft and flexible.

• Since your thumb will be resting on harmonics in this book, it is not required that you firmly stop the strings with the thumb. However, I usually recommend that you try to balance some weight from your back onto the thumb. That way it will remain in one spot on the string and not wander around the harmonic spot. Be sure that you do not collapse your knuckles or tighten your thumb as you do this.

Here are a few practice hints:

• The Daily Warm-ups at the beginning of each section are designed to help you establish each finger pattern carefully and correctly. Please practice them slowly with careful attention to intonation. Practice them every day, but don't feel that you must finish all of them before starting on the pieces.

• As you play the pieces, notice the names of the notes and the distances between them so you will know which finger pattern you must use. Then pay attention to how each pattern feels. If you memorize the feelings, you can successfully use these patterns in other pieces.

• You will notice that there are very few fingerings in this book. That is because your hand will remain basically in the same place on the fingerboard all the time. Since there is no shifting, you should be able to figure out the fingerings for yourself.

• In addition to the fast fiddle tunes in this book, I have included several pieces in each section which are slow and melodic. Please try to vibrato on these pieces. Using a mellow, relaxed vibrato will help make sure that your hand stays loose and balanced.

I hope you enjoy playing these pieces. I really believe that developing good technique can be a lot of fun!

-- Rick Mooney

Thumb Position Pattern I
half step between 2nd and 3rd fingers

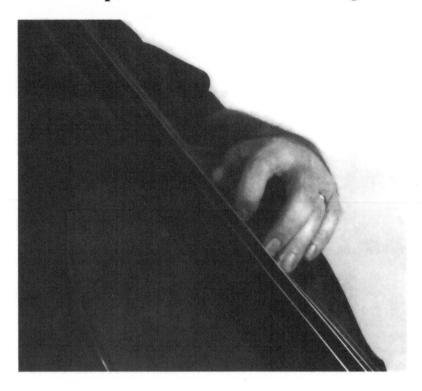

Daily Warm-ups

Thumb Position for Cello

Book 1

by Rick Mooney

© 1998 Summy-Birchard Music
a division of Summy-Birchard, Inc.
Exclusive print rights administered by
Alfred Publishing Co., Inc.
All rights reserved.   Printed in USA.

0-87487-763-6

Contents

Thumb Position Pattern I -- Daily Warm-ups (continued)

French Folk Song

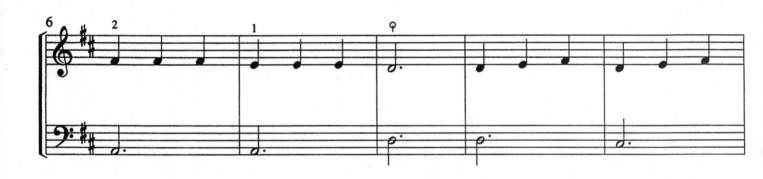

May Song
(Alle Vögel Sind Schon Da)

Oh Susannah

Stephen Foster

Are You Sleeping?

(Frère Jacques)

I'll Always Remember You

Rick Mooney

Soldier's Joy

Arkansas Traveller

Arkansas Traveller

The Hundred Pipers

The Hundred Pipers

The Hundred Pipers

Thumb Position Pattern II
half step between 1st and 2nd fingers

Daily Warm-ups

Thumb Position Pattern II -- Daily Warm-ups (continued)

French Folk Song

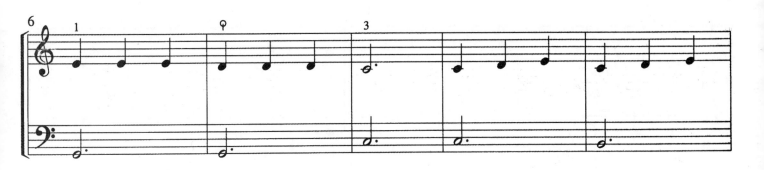

May Song
(Alle Vögel Sind Schon Da)

Oh Susannah

Stephen Foster

Old Folks at Home

Stephen Foster

The Blue Bells of Scotland

Crawdad

The Devil's Dream

The California Traveller

Rick Mooney

Thumb Position Pattern III
half step between thumb and 1st finger

Daily Warm-ups

Thumb Position Pattern III -- Daily Warm-ups (continued)

French Folk Song

May Song
(Alle Vögel Sind Schon Da)

Oh Susannah

Stephen Foster

Cockles and Mussels

Larry O'Gaff

Battle Hymn of the Republic

Fisher's Hornpipe

The Piper of Dundee

Fine

The Piper of Dundee

Thumb Position Pattern IV
no half steps

Daily Warm-ups

Thumb Position Pattern IV -- Daily Warm-ups (continued)

French Folk Song

May Song
(Alle Vögel Sind Schon Da)

Oh Susannah

Stephen Foster

Clair de Lune

My Wild Irish Rose

Garry Owen

Eat My Dust

Rick Mooney

Minuet

J. S. Bach

Rigadoon

Henry Purcell

48

Rigadoon

Old French Song

P. I. Tchaikowsky

German Dance

P. I. Tchaikowsky

Highland Hoedown

Highland Hoedown

Highland Hoedown

Chorale
Brich Entzwei, Mein Armes Herze

J. S. Bach

The Irish Washerwoman

Go Down, Moses

Chorale
Gott, Wie Gross Ist Deine Güte

J. S. Bach

poco rit.

Walking Music from Appelbo
(Gånglåt Från Äppelbo)

The Coyote's Bark

Rick Mooney

The Coyote's Bark

Chorale
Die Bittre Leidenszeit

J. S. Bach

Die Bittre Leidenszeit

Chorale
Jesu, Deine Liebeswunden

J. S. Bach

Boil Them Cabbage Down

Boil Them Cabbage Down

Boil Them Cabbage Down

Chorale
Jesu, Jesu, Du Bist Mein

J. S. Bach

The Triumph

The Triumph

The Triumph

The Triumph